T0094656

DAVID MCGIMPSEY

ASBESTOS HEIGHTS

THE CANONICAL NOTEBOOKS

Coach House Books, Toronto

Canada Council **Conseil des Arts**
for the Arts **du Canada**

Published with the generous assistance of the Canada Council for the Arts
and the Ontario Arts Council. Coach House Books also acknowledges the
support of the Government of Canada through the Canada Book Fund and
the Government of Ontario through the Ontario Book Publishing Tax Credit.

LIBRARY AND ARCHIVES CANADA CATALOGUING IN PUBLICATION

McGimpsey, David, author
        Asbestos Heights / David McGimpsey.

Poems.
Issued in print and electronic formats.
ISBN 978-1-55245-309-4 (pbk.)

        I. Title.

PS8575.G48A73 2015   C811'.54   C2014-908355-6

Asbestos Heights is available as an ebook: ISBN 978 1 77056 415 2

Purchase of the print version of this book entitles you to a free digital copy.
To claim your ebook of this title, please email sales@ chbooks.com with
proof of purchase or visit chbooks.com/ digital. (Coach House Books reserves
the right to terminate the free digital download offer at any time.)

for my father, John McGimpsey

all the flowers in Ville D'Anjou
& the New York Yankees.

NOTEBOOK I

A HARKENING OF FLOWERS

'Hath sorrow struck so many blows upon this face of mine
and made no deeper wounds?' – Richard II

Some drink grappa in Old Trieste
Some publish novels with a vanity press
But I love noodles

Some name their country homes 'Le BelleBelle Rive'
Some name their yachts 'O Big Mighty Steve'
But I love noodles

Some like the taste of mackerel in a can
Some can't write essays without quoting Lacan
But I love noodles

Some like to consider nude curling the hardest sport
Some like to call the tansy flower common yellow mugwort
But I love noodles

Some love a poem that speaks of rare flowers
Some wake up and say, 'Ohmigod! Gotta shower!'
But I love noodles

Lettuce

For poetry's sake, let us consider
iceberg lettuce a flower, much as I
considered (for poetry's sake) college
a place where I would find value in life.

I can't say whether or not my whole year
was good for bouquets of iceberg lettuce,
blooming in beds of bacon and mayonnaise,
just that I remember their quiet, cold heads.

Stamen, anther, filament – I clammed up
for most of the summer. It wasn't so bad.
I missed the old provocations of rage,
moved on, and didn't gain too much weight.

Imagine the bride is holding her lettuce
and, then, tosses it to the eager crowd.
For poetry's sake, I really have to say
I am happy for her among the crispy petals.

Lichen

What I remember about the lichen
were its inevitable invasions.
It would cover Taco Bell franchises
if you didn't respect it and kill it.

Dogwood blossoms were different, I think.
In April, in Georgia, I could smell them
while looking up to the sky, calling
any scramble of stars *Sagittarius*.

From April came May and then other months
that also demonstrated my general facility
with the Gregorian calendar. By October,
I was puking all the cow grass I ate.

Lichen is a perfect combination
of algae and fungus, whereas we were
the perfect combination of liver
and peaches. We sure were a freezerful.

Scarlet Geraniums

A beach towel I bought in Barcelona
had a crest of scarlet geraniums.
Who would I give that to besides the one
I didn't give the Kim Kardashian towel to?

Scarlet geraniums are not natural
to Ville D'Anjou, Quebec. 'You're amazing,
but you will always hurt those who fall
for your charm. You won't mean to, but you will.'

The cover of Ted Hughes's *Birthday Letters*
has a similar strew of geraniums,
but he wasted no time singing his anthem,
'This One Goes out to the One I Fucked Up.'

I bought duty-free Iberian ham
rather than beach gear, which only affirmed
the Spanish maxim: *You always end up*
eating the Iberian ham you love.

Blackberry

Eventually, my critique was refined to
'I hope all you sickening snobs just die.'
I ate blackberries every morning (once)
and held on to my earned, mature insight.

What people generally liked about me
was the thought they could do my job.
The quality my closest friends loved most
was that I was 'a generous tipper.'

I read on some site blackberries were good
for the lungs. I knew they tasted really weird.
Fruits that taste good have soda pops based on them.
Isn't that right, Diet Sierra Mist Kiwi?

Did I mention all the blackberry smoothies
and drinking them in one gulp, imagining
I was steadying myself on Jesus's shoulder?
Jesus, of course, would just have Diet Sprite.

Canola Flowers

If you tore off the tops of canola –
yellow canola flowers – would you
jump in a tub of canola margarine
just to make the best of despair?

Do you miss those bed-bound Sundays we had?
You'd read classic American novels
and when it was Henry James you would scream
at the heroine, 'Oh, just bend over!'

Into the acacia you go, scowl mouth.
Into the acacia with you, whatever
Jonathan Franzen novel with the girl
who chews the cuffs of her new blue blouse.

Like *heartfelt, canola* is a made-up word.
It brings together *Canada* and *oil*.
It's a tub of fun you'll be glad to call
I Can't Believe It's Not More Meaningful.

Columbines

In the kingdom *Plantae*, in the 'You stink,
Ophelia' class, four of five columbines
mark the spot where I finally decided
to increase my social media profile.

O, Annie Facebook, Clarissa Twitter -
we're going to the prom! I shed real tears
just because my poem for Beyoncé
was rejected by the *Malahat Review*.

Could the columbines be mashed into scent,
giving me a resilient mountain freshness?
The answer, after that long flight to Paris,
was a resounding *absolutement pas*.

Still, I knew I was going to pluck and pluck,
and I plucked until plucking became my life,
well beyond any interest in sowing
and its much-funner cousin reaping.

Tulips

Corduroy once ruled the kingdom of pants.
I was still writing poetry back then.
Or, whatever it was I did back then
that made people say, 'That's not poetry!'

The tulips my father planted back home
bloomed steady most Easter-times, sure as
the plans I sketched out to start feeling good
got crumpled alongside a map to Rome.

Casting 'foul light upon neighbouring ponds'
was not my cup of Sprite, but I enjoyed
choking with anxiety whenever
the seasons made a definitive change.

Fall was all university khakis
and old Nantuckets braying, 'Hey, Corduroy!
Your footgame burger garbage is garbage!'
until it was finally footgame season.

Nasturtium

I took careful notes on the nasturtiums,
ticking off each one I saw. Over the year –
year and a half? – I saw near six hundred.
The best and dumbest thing I ever did.

As long as it rains, nasturtiums will grow
and the cycle of life, from grassy spore
to Mars Incorporated's decision
to make pina colada M&Ms, will go on.

Oh, through it all, nose after heady nose,
racking up scores, I started to lose heart;
it sounds fancy and fragrant, when, really,
I couldn't be bothered with instant soup.

Bring primrose like tomato soup
and jasmine like a fresh oyster chowder;
O daffodilly-coloured chicken noodle,
O nasturtium with cloved pumpkin flower.

Johnson's Blue Geranium

As late I returned to that corner café,
so favoured by Montreal hipsters;
I could not tell any of my old friends
what happened after that stinky summer.

It was spring and I spotted what I thought
were Instagrammable crocuses
but were, I was told, Siberian squills
or maybe Johnson's blue geraniums.

Traditionally, blue geraniums
symbolize a gentle constancy,
where the Siberian squill represents
being murdered by Joseph Stalin.

I would have eaten them all, like a cow,
just to ease the pain of not knowing.
I returned to that corner cafe squinting,
having long run out of quelling lies.

(*after Keats*)

Lady's Slipper

That poem was my career. It poured flop sweat
and begged grad students to stop hating me.
It punched at the famous and took cover
in weeks of Beyoncé-fed solitude.

That poem knew where it was and how much
it was worth compared to a blow job.
It knew the other poems by name: they
gave me panic attacks they struck so quick.

That poem was the great hope I wouldn't work
for a living, the dream I could survive,
being admired as if an academic
John Stamos (or a telegenic Žižek).

That poem did what I told it to do.
Sort of. It snarled up on Asbestos Heights.
Now, of course, snarling is all it's good for
as my hunchback moves to the left, to the left.

Saffron

When the Glooscap Trail in Nova Scotia
got too Glooscappy for me, I turned south.
All the buckeyes and all the baseball games
I'd need to score to prove I didn't mind.

Not that I grew so blessed with freedom
I outlived personifying the wind
(it 'murmured,' it 'howled,' it even 'bled')
or outlived those who spoke for literature.

Wherever they were, every sentence began
'Poetry is … ' and zeroed in, like a hawk,
to how foolish it was I spent seven years
writing sonnets about orange soda pop.

My lungs were born to proof asbestos,
my teeth edged to tear open Doritos.
Poetry was bound to love Nova Scotia,
what with its winds singing Taylor Swift songs.

Pomegranate

There are two kinds of people in the world:
those who say they love to eat pomegranates
and those who tell the truth. But, yes, they're red,
and healthy foods taste either red or red.

Steak, cherry popsicle, red velvet cake.
Full of such health, I stayed up all summer
sketching a fringe play called *Dangling Apricocks*
and collapsing somewhere near Jolicoeur.

When somebody looks over their glasses and says,
'Look at it this way, *m'sieur*, you have a scar
but at least you still have most of your face,'
what can you say but 'D'you like daiquiris?'

Healthy red medicines, or even those blushed
Pepto pink, die in the Canadian cold;
you can't keep Diet Cokes at home for fear
the deliciousness will dull you to God.

Yarrow

There's the country somewhere outside the car.
The country where the elm fucks the maple
and the elm broods as if auditioning
for a new PBS miniseries.

There's a poetry where trees don't have sex,
when the yarrow observed from a car seat
can stand in, plain image, plain symbol,
and not be you observing me as overweight.

Outside, as the yarrow whips by, are towns
where Canadians happily live their lives,
unperturbed by who was excluded
from the *Can Lit? Can Do!* anthology.

Inside, the steady beat of country songs,
coffee with diet hazelnut creamer.
Maybe I shouldn't have said anything
about the maple who gets so leafy.

Queen Anne's Lace

My therapist looked over her glasses.
'I hate it when you say that nobody cares
if you live or die when I, for one, am
quite excited by the idea of you dying.'

I stared at her desk bouquet of Queen Anne's lace,
wondering when we would talk about drinking.
How happy I was to know I'd leave there,
go to my pub and tell jokes to Cakeface.

I told her about the walks in the mall,
how happy I was just to sit and read –
except reading Frank Norris, of course –
I mean, who on earth could be happy then?

'Why are you telling me this?' she said,
tacking back to more analytical words.
'No matter how devoted to my job,
I would never read one of your books'!

Sunflower

Like a foul-tempered baseball manager
observing the bumbles of his hapless nine,
I obsessively ate sunflower seeds.
Chewing and spitting. Spitting and chewing.

In winter, as I walked home from college,
roughed up by the hilarious comments
about my appearance, my strategy
was soon limited to 'eat lots of seeds.'

Of course, it didn't help I had the pride
of Richard II. It didn't help I switched
from sunflower seeds to popcorn chicken
and from popcorn chicken to popcorn steak.

I didn't need another reviewer
who hated 'frivolity' to tell me
I was losing all *Bunyon Review* cred,
and that all things from Kansas made him sick.

Basil

The discovery of the basil plant was not
made by British actor Basil Rathbone,
but by an ordinary guy from Boston
who was just still Basil from the block.

It was, as they say in the plant-birth biz,
'licorice-y.' Not really your kind of thing,
you confessed, after saying I 'made up'
that 'stuff about humans needing affection.'

You can't hate someone for saying 'We were
together for a long time, but were we,
like, ever, really together?,' but it sure
helps you appreciate arena football.

I learned to hate basil, called it *buttfool*,
delaware parsley, poor man's toback,
while I sat weeping in Old Navy pants.
It's hard to hate wearing Old Navy pants.

Snowdrop

These are the parts of east coast manuscripts
where a robin (or crested goshawk)
takes its beak and just starts jackhammering
your ass with messages of winter hope.

It's okay. I get it. If I say I feel
like having jellyhearts that doesn't mean
we'll be having jellyhearts anytime soon
(no more jellyhearts on Jellyhearts' Eve).

This is the part where I'm supposed to get up,
visit Italy, get Julia-Roberts strong,
then smite my enemies – cleverly disguised
as more than three thousand Facebook friends.

Just call me Dr. Argyle Sweater Vest.
The bloom of the snowdrop faces downward,
like a long lineup's bashful supplicant
who finds consolation in the worst news.

Aster

Itchier than an itch begging outside
the Lanacane factory, lonely as a boner
working a disco in Gore-Tex pants,
I still had the patience for baseball.

I used to drive from Montreal to New York.
Past the red hots of the Adirondacks,
by the little hot dogs of the Mohawk Valley,
to the coney dogs around Yankee Stadium.

The asters on the roadside banks, wispy blurs,
could be squeezed one day from the roots up
to draw out at least three Canadian poems,
but until then I would just have baseball.

Ready as Reddi-wip but unwilling
to do much but pray God helps the Yankees.
The lesson of American Literature,
after all, is just drive until you're alone.

Mustard

I parodied Tennyson's *Locksley Hall*,
as if the speaker were a dinosaur:
'O Percy Triceratops! O Percy!
O dreary swampnose! O dear Percybone!'

Sounds bad and it wasn't even that good.
Still, at the time, I was hurt my dinos
at Victoria's gate were not as loved
as that poem about Grampa's rare coins.

No, those were not coins used in automats.
They were octagonal, iodine-stained,
embossed with moustached dictators,
clutched in line while waiting for winter soup.

Years later, of course, I accepted it.
I knew Dinosaur Nell was just saying:
better a day as cauliflower broth
than millennia as ballpark mustard.

Orange Poppies

There's no Nixon-goes-to-China move left.
No tale my pink, Kennedy-sized head
doesn't tell you without your asking.
In French it's called *Rue de la End, My Friend*.

I went into debt renting hotel rooms,
my longest conversation with the front desk:
'Yes, I am going to stay three more days,
reruns of *Cheers* in the north of England!'

Much like a Maupassant story, I think,
I worked hard to erase my debts, and then,
my face, bashed by age and east-end doctors –
oh, poppies, lilies and chrysanthemums.

Mark Twain's rock-bottom memoir of being drunk
and slinking through the dusty back streets
of Virginia City, unseen, alone,
seems like a late-life paradise to me.

Lungwort

Pale forget-me-nots outside an Arby's
in Canoga Park. Byron's Valley,
'Without the farce of friendship or romance
of Platonism,' held up all winter.

After my surgery, my hair went white
and I forgot about my novel draft
and the fortune of its protagonists,
Acetaminophen and Ibuprofen.

One person's honest evaluation
is another person's snark, one person's
seriousness is another person's
burlesque. One's love is another's CHUD.

I missed Montreal, though. Its slush piles,
its cemeteries and its 'mystery cheques.'
Who cares of a flower's resolve to bloom
once you have a head start on the ice age?

NOTEBOOK II

THE HISTORY OF BASEBALL

'A few prosaic days / A little this side of the snow'
– Emily Dickinson

Some like a wine with a hit of applewood
Some like to call a dude 'Mr. Dude'
But I love noodles

Some like their Mariners without ancient rime
Some like the chances of the Mudville Nine
But I love noodles

Some like their vengeance served without scorn
Some like a cheese in delightful string form
But I love noodles

Some love to tell you, 'Just try to act classy'
Some like their Philip Glass a little extra glassy
But I love noodles

Anne Bradstreet

When composing literary biography,
predictive text takes care of the phrase
'born a sickly child.' But the writer's free
to note details of an albino fox.

It's not known if Anne Bradstreet played golf,
despite her instrumental role in securing
the plot where golf wear and golf-club manners
would be understood by happy readers.

Baseball is a kind of golf, a kind of
zeppelin race and a kind of arithmetic
that adds the names of horses so hungry
they've resorted to eating each others' tails.

Bradstreet's wiki reads, 'America's first
Houston Astros fan, big-boned futurist,
believed Abner Doubleday a time traveller
out to kill the inventors of football.'

Michael Wigglesworth

Anne Bradstreet worked as a stand-up comic
under the name Goody B. Her act was mostly
'Puritans are, like, "Thank God"; Non-Puritans
are, like, "Let's swim in the hot blood of swine!"'

Her rival, Michael 'Wiggly' Wigglesworth,
was mostly 'Puritans are, like, 'I Love You,
Jesus'; Non-Puritans are, like, 'I'm fine
with the devil lacerating my face!"

The baseball game they once caught together,
Salem Witches vs. New Haven Nutmegs,
proved a point that became foundational:
with more Bud Light, more Bud Light's required.

Years later, when people would say things like
'The Church of Baseball' without vomiting,
all records of my cancer surgery
were locked in a coffin called *Coffinboy*.

William Bartram

Where the peaches grow, the peaches grow
into a source of reusable fuel.
Where deer kidney could also power engines
if deer kidney didn't taste so much like plum.

The Chumgut River is pallid and cold.
Lingering through April to play a game
of Oak Hearts – where wet tree pulp is bashed
by pine beams for first go at the town jug.

O the industries that will grow one day!
The shoe industry! The shoe support industry!
The shoe support industrial complex:
poems and novels about shoesome shoes.

Novels have characters named *Mendifort,*
poems have *skin kissed into turmeric glow.*
Games of Oak Hearts have an immediate rush,
under the sky, and let's not forget that jug.

Henry Wadsworth Longfellow

Let's be clear. I'm going to towel-snap you
out of the way. Don't act like you don't know.
Please don't pretend you don't have it coming.
You may be late for your game of Blue Jays.

Baseball is great without your poetry.
Check the Vegas over/under on how
often poets will use the word *Corona*
and not mean the beer and take the over!

I'm not getting better. I can make fun
of how my doctor looks like Lurch all I want.
It doesn't light lanterns in the Old North Church
or make me think your face isn't stupid.

If I were to start praying, it would not be
for my life. It would be that the Yankees
win yet another World Series Championship.
It's an insult to pray for the impossible.

Washington Irving

Poor Rip was asleep when townsfolk told him
Derek Jeter had retired. Poor Rip
clutched his gun, didn't hear how each home run
ever hit was hit in his honour.

Every scratch in every game-day scorecard
refers to Rip Van Winkle, even when
I wrote in the margin, 'I have to go back
to teaching. Dreams don't just crush themselves.'

The falling maples leaves, Dame Van Winkle,
bring us both back to freshman year, never
dressed quite right for the coming cold, never
stopping to tour the nutmeg factory.

I hated Halloween and Hallowinkle.
I once sang, 'You'll be a hot dog woman,
baby, till you find a ham,' ready to play,
dressed up as a pudgy Leslie Fiedler.

Ralph Waldo Emerson

If Ronald Reagan never existed,
Emerson would have invented him.
'Here's a man who will invent swimming pools
and will jackknife into bald-eagle soup.'

Emerson, however, would hate baseball,
particularly if he had the sense
there would be a franchise in Atlanta
and Larry Jones's nickname would be Chipper.

The truth is, actually, nothing denies
the authority of an intellectual life
like the body: big hit, nice waist, strong arm,
pretty hair, fat man falls on the queen.

Emerson's immunity to the condition
that would be known in literary circles
as 'Looking Toronto' is worth noting.
Nobody needs to know what a bunt is.

Walt Whitman

Whitman saw great things in the 'game of base'
and predicted that one day there'd be a team
in Albany called the Angel-Snappers
who would play shirtless in the summer sun.

When the rules disallowed 'soaking'
(throwing a runner out by throwing at him),
the fun of Whitman's game was gone,
and he died good in Camden, New Jersey.

Nineteenth-century baseball, as you know,
featured spectacular mustachio play
and ad endorsements were for 'stropping,'
'hamboiling,' 'stonerail fixing' and 'unsnaking.'

Whitman's baseball rap has no real substance,
of course; his thoughts on the game exist
to comfort all washed-up peanut-tossers,
long assured they were unfit for poetry.

Emily Dickinson

The fact there are so many good poems
about baseball is just further proof
that A) nobody cares about poetry
and B) they care even less about your poetry.

'The Rules of baseball Buzzed by like a fly —
as Nobody Went to bat for Bizarro Jesus,'
wrote an Amherst, Massachusetts, author,
still thinking she might be published one day.

The Amherst Arrows didn't last too long.
Though many made sour pork in aspic
for Amherst Arrow picnics, the Arrows left
and became the Jersey City Skeeters.

'The Skeeters stood like they Were dead — / And I
ate Lots of Pie — / They said I Wasn't Fit
for Harvard / But I really Tried,' she wrote
in a newsletter for a peanut factory.

Herman Melville

The greatest baseball novel is *Moby-Dick*.
Not because Captain Ahab reminds me
of Gene Mauch, but because Starbuck's perfect
for all Kevin Costner moralisms.

The New Bedford Nine's Race for the Pennant.
The Boys of the Whale-Killing Summer.
The Big Game and Stabbing an Albino Whale
Right in Its Fucking Stupid Whaley Eye.

Baseball novels usually start with abjection –
I found myself riding the Pequod's pines –
and through body-comedy find victory
or loss. 'Funny, but is it writing?'

Given the ivory tower's ivoriness,
and its persistent monocle-related
injuries, it's easy to understand
hostility to Herman 'Babe' Melville.

Mark Twain

Mark Twain's own daughter would privately wish
that her father would write 'serious books'
so stinkers who wrote him off as lowbrow
would see how brilliant he actually was.

Trying to explain the rules of baseball
to King Arthur's Court is a comedy skit,
not too different than my trying to sell a poem
about Urkel to the *Denver Quarterly*.

Of course, co-hosting a radio show
for two years to mock the Boston Red Sox
wasn't exactly *Huckleberry Finn*.
It wasn't even Cher's 'Tug It, BoSox.'

Comedies don't win Oscars, nor do they win
Employee of the Month at El Pollo Loco
in Houston. For having a book with the word
Pudd'nhead in the title, Twain was dead serious.

Edith Wharton

The mysteries of life don't reveal themselves
because you threaten to write a poem.
You don't just rub your eyes on Broadway
and see Fatso's Pizza and Weepy's Tavern.

Mme. Olenska was proud but, you know, well,
'she was lonely and she was unhappy.'
Likewise, I praised a book's use of apostrophe
then I said, 'Peanuts right here! Bud Light too!'

Fiction's dream is you'll survive a subway ride,
poetry blames the poor for leukemia.
Poetry sees a baseball on a hilltop,
fiction sees the skin on your soup is gross.

When my colleagues knew my poems
were pulled from the final edition
but acted sweet to me at the poets' lunch,
that's an example of *dramatic irony*.

Kate Chopin

I was going to mention how Kate Chopin
raised beagles and say her favourite was Lefty
which, coincidentally, is the most
popular baseball nickname of all time.

But, of course, that's not true. Also not true:
Kate Chopin's nickname was Katie-Chops.
Chopin lived until fifty-two (that's old)
and felt great pain at how she was dismissed.

However, her classic, *The Awakening*,
has this omen of the lover's impotence:
'a little finger which he can't straighten
from having played baseball too energetically.'

If there really was a Lefty the Beagle
he'd be sleeping nearby right now.
And Lefty would ask, 'Why you want people
to hate baseball like they hate poetry?'

Marianne Moore

Marianne Moore was the best on baseball
insofar as she was an actual fan.
Fields of green are fine, but they don't stack up
against watching your team win on TV.

Moore's actual writing on baseball is *meh*,
Brooklyn Trolleydodger doggerel *meh*,
the inevitable *meh* of comparing the sport
to writing because *oh boy, writing, oh boy!*

But, as the Bible asks, 'For whom
hath a more pitiful existence than he
whose neighbour is learning to play
clarinet?' It's not the end of the world.

Many writers are baseball fans. Literature
and sports are products eagerly consumed
by millions. You don't have to take a test.
You just have to cheer for some team to win.

Ernest Hemingway

I'd never pray to Jesus, but I'd say
the novena of grace for Fat Batman.
Most amiable, loving Fat Batman,
let the Yankees win this World Series.

Hemingway constructed Santiago
(literature's greatest Yankees fan,
ergo the greatest character in literature)
with Steinbrennerian eye to result.

Clouds can be 'friendly piles of ice cream,'
but the Yanks do not drift to Hemingway.
Baseball players have no superpowers,
and Santiago is as dead as the next.

Il est certainement nécessaire d'apprendre
la doctrine enseignée par Batman-Gros –
I implore thee, Fat Batman, let the great
DiMaggio be heard in Asbestos Heights.

F. Scott Fitzgerald

Gatsby studied the manners of baseball
to 'fit in.' The best way to fit into baseball
is to go to the track in Saratoga,
and – Kobayashi Maru – fix the World Series.

I grew up anglophone in French Quebec.
The neighbors looked at me and said, '*Vers l'enfers,
mon ennemi héréditaire!*' which means
'Dear friend, you're welcome to live in peace.'

My mother made me a steak for my first
Little League game, which might as well have been
Excelsiors versus Knickerbockers
in some sunlit Manhattan cricket patch.

I think the best way to fit into Quebec
is to not think it that different from Cleveland.
At least that seemed plausible with the Expos,
when you coped as others did: with alcohol.

William Faulkner

One out of every thousand Hart Cranes
does not commit suicide. Tough odds, sure,
but a lot better than the odds of throwing
a perfect game for the Chicago Cubs.

One out of every seven Philip Roths
gets sent a card on his birthday that says,
'Dude, totally great joke about the guy
whacking off into the catcher's mitt!'

One out of one William Faulkners tells me,
'When it comes to squandering all friendships,
when summers are too hot for baseball,
the smart money's still on the Anjou Kid!'

Faulkner, taking his cabbage at Musso's,
was also the one out of the one Faulkners
not buying this. Contrary to book-club myth,
he actually really loved Hollywood.

Saul Bellow

Nobody cruising to thirty home runs,
a hundred RBIS, is thinking,
'I hope my creative writing professor
likes my poem about writing poems.'

Saul Bellow's Moses Herzog's 'fuckyknuckles'
were the excuse for why he, man enough,
still wasn't cut for baseball. Fair enough.
Nobody leaves baseball for literature.

Delmore Schwartz, the real Von Humboldt Fleisher
in Saul Bellow's roman à clef *Humboldt's Gift*,
despairingly wondered why poetry
couldn't excite him the way the Giants did.

It hurts he couldn't consider how the Giants
were having a better season than poetry,
and one day MFA programs would admit
all the fuckyknucklers they could handle.

Jack Kerouac

Lefty Murphree manned the seven spot
for the Philadelphia Pontiacs,
a fantasy team invented by Jack Kerouac,
played with cards and a Parcheesi board.

Reluctant to leave what he called 'the sad
peasant mysticism of Quebec Catholics,'
Kerouac rode out the hard part of life
in his mother's house, drunk on canned beer.

I imagine the New York Chevies still field
a reasonable nine, and Zagg Parker,
from center, can clearly see that poetry's
a crease in a forehead made by a top hat.

Poetry's a social activity, the golf club
outside the game of golf. It's not complex,
it's the kind of place where social injustice
is blamed on your failure to love David Byrne.

Norman Mailer

The ball is blasted through the poem, kiddo.
If you didn't want to see fence-clearing dingers,
why would you take the time to kiss Babe Ruth
and buy *The Short Right Field Porch of Prose*?

Why would most of your old friends take the time
to passive-aggressively freeze you out?
Did they not buy boxers at Superior Park
just to shout, 'Hit one out, Jimmy McClout!'

The ball finally sails above the poem, its spin
stuck in words that mean 'flying jizz,' whereas
a copy of *The Flying Jizz Poems* is inscribed
'My signature is punishment enough.'

Slugged over the fence every single time,
the ball's like a poem if it gets an A,
sits down to brunch, complains about Kansas,
screams, 'That's a goddamned home run, you cocks!'

Thomas Pynchon

Loving something that doesn't love you back
is the beginning of your relationship
with God. Learning to love baseball is fun –
Bud Light funbo-fun, swatted balls funzo-fun.

It was like a Bible camp punishment
to talk of Thomas Pynchon in grad school.
Pynchon's heat-death, they said, awaited me
if I continued eating Expoghetti.

The 'noise' of the world was too much for them;
as if Ivory Soap, Porky Pig cartoons,
supermarket booze and Perry Mason
could drown out their poems about Nixon.

I missed the Expos when I had a school
reading. Oh, God, my creative writing
professor introduced me, noting 'how lean'
my words were compared to how fat my body.

Sylvia Plath

I can't quite distinguish Sylvia Plath
from Sarah Palin and can't distinguish
Sylvia Plath from how Tina Fey played
Plath in the SNL skit 'Sad Sivvie.'

I don't recognize my own face. One day
a punk kid, stunned by the jacket photos
of admired poets, the next looking more
beardy and blind than John Berryman.

Plath imagined her art's insensitive foils
as the 'peanut crunchers' around ball games.
When I spoke of my dream trip visiting ballparks,
my poetry teacher said, 'What a nightmare!'

My father, at ninety-nine, could not
recognize his favourite Yankees' faces
but knew their body shapes, averages
and what they did their last time at bat.

NOTEBOOK III

A HISTORY OF CANADA:
ITS POETRY, ITS BIRDS, ITS PRIME
MINISTERS AND ITS TREES

'Mais que devient le rêveur / Quand le rêve est fini?'
– Hubert-Félix Thiéfaine

Some like a poem when they're sorting fine china
Some like their jambalaya with a little less balaya
But I love noodles

Some like a hip that echoes the moves of Danny Terrio
Some like to tickle the balls of Southern Ontario
But I love noodles

Some wouldn't budge for all the ham in Spain
Some use more exclamation marks than Shania Twain
But I love noodles

Some sing 'O Canada!' without a care
Some stash loonies in their underwear
But I love noodles

**'I would never go myself because, you know, I have the
internet, but I hear that Montreal's Botanical Gardens
is a nice place to visit!'**

At the age of forty-five I started
teaching Canadian Literature.
My students learned to bow their heads and sing,
'The soul of the suburbs is in my toes.'

I met all the great writers nobody
outside Canada has heard of: Burksome,
McAllister, Fatchett, Stemens and Donk.
Not a well-dressed crew but, you know, sincere.

I watched nature shows on the internet
and lived east, near the Place Versailles mall,
took afternoon coffee in the food court,
and graded papers. 'C for Canada!'

'Mais, vous avez un accent américain!'
I'd been to the Del Taco in Barstow,
I'd been to the Del Taco in Roseville,
It was time to retire in Montreal.

I always wanted to die every time somebody said
something like 'Poetry is like dancing with a shadow'
so I can't say I never had any feelings for poetry.

My interest in Canadian poetry
is firmly rooted in my teenage years.
I studied classical music but, still,
poets were the most enviably dead.

It was easy to give up on baseball,
but still frustratingly hard to give up
on friendship. But, somehow, with poetry,
I was finally able to do just that!

In music, I had a sense of *repertoire*.
On the mound, I had four reliable pitches:
a fastball (which may've been my weakest)
and three different kinds of spitballs.

With much less to rely on, I moved on.
I studied poems fixedly in college,
thinking one day I would see my name
beside some of those groovy suicides.

'Switching back and forth between academic and literary publishing will be as easy as dancing on the hood of a car,' or so it says in the latest *Quarterly Review of White Snake Videos.*

I am not afraid of coast-to-coast flights.
The app that converts Pacific Time
for west coast residents automatically converts
Kafka quotes to lyrics by the Eagles.

You can be justly proud of your thoughts on Pound,
but a working scholar learns to respect
TLC for not recording 'These Days,
Gotta Say, I'd Totally Settle for a Scrub.'

Bruce Springsteen's hit song 'Millionaire Onion'
may not be Bruce Springsteen's greatest song
but it's definitely his best song about
an onion who is also a millionaire.

'*The millionaire onion came into town /
The millionaire onion closed the factories down.*'
If you saw your professors' clothes and said,
'This is my life!,' then, yeah, zero sympathy.

Aw ya, rancheros y rancheras, it's time for a little polling data about everybody's favourite subject, Canadian Literature!

The luckiest character in CanLit
has to be David from Earle Birney's 'David'
because David would be safely dead
before having to read Earle Birney's 'David.'

The most beloved character in CanLit
is, for sure, Chanis MacGovernor
from *The MacGovernor Tales*, the thrifty
merchant who 'taught Canada how to save!'

The most grateful characters in CanLit
are all the ones not named Morag,
while the saddest ones are the characters
who've never had sex with Leonard Cohen.

The sexiest character in CanLit
would have to be be either Reverend Cocksome
from *Niagara Love* or Poundy DeLaGrace
from *Destin du Pays, Destin d'Ohhh.*

As vast as the vastlands of this vast land, poet, are you to yonder skies, breads and local cheeses.

I am grateful for libraries (iPad)
and poetry (iPad). Lorca's line
'*La Clooney del bello Jorge sigue ...*'
is where George Clooney got his stage name.

Many tried to be 'The Lorca of Canada'
but stopped when being 'The Octavio Paz
of Sault Ste. Marie' proved sufficient.
Entre la tarde Timbits y la noche.

Life in Canada is just bear attack
after bear attack. It always happens,
as incalculable as the number of times
Irving Layton used the word *loins*.

In the animal kingdom, no creature
kills for sport except the otter.
In the plant world, there are few things
as objectionable as balsam fir.

Those who do not learn their history are condemned to not have an opinion as to what Sir John A. Macdonald's favourite Justin Bieber song would have been.

Beyoncé reads about a jaguar's health.
It's been four months since she kinda gave up
on the collection *A Clatter of Hooves:*
Canadian Poetry's Biggest Poem-Makers.

Beyoncé's library, from the pictures,
seems to be in Houston, but a Houston
with more electric cars and fewer people
saying, 'Oh, yeah, where's that gonna get you?'

All libraries are credible ripostes
to conversations that hold us down
and smother us. 'I am sorry for your
many cancers and for that Sting concert.'

Why bother knocking when you plan to break down
the door? Jaguars live only in poems –
'Aunt Juniper's Jaguars' or some such hoot
that Houston would never bother with.

Mon pays c'est ne pas un pays c'est $100 pour voir Bon Iver.

Oddsmakers ask, what will happen sooner:
will a Canadian team win the Stanley Cup
or will Canadians develop new interest
in the novels of Robertson Davies?

The unmalled parts of Edmonton are cold,
my friend, and for reasons I don't know,
the Cinnabon franchises in Montreal closed,
giving the city the nickname *Russia*.

Limited atonement, one of the five points
of Calvinism, is what Canadians
think of as 'catnip.' Heaven is the ground
where the Winnipeg Victorias still play.

I, of course, have never read *Fifth Business*,
because pop music is better. But, unlike
the speaker of Rod Stewart's 'Maggie May,'
I definitely could have tried a lot more.

You may remember me from the small-press Canadian poetry titles *Sugar Shack Parson* **and** *Midnight Call to Petawawa.*

Bilingualism in Quebec is fine
but Montreal suit sellers don't know English
well enough to avoid certain sad-making
euphemisms for *fat.* They say *big* and *fat.*

The French translation of *The Clockmaker*
is called *Le Tic Toc.* In Nova Scotia,
sales of *Le Tic Toc* came with a warning:
Adult-Orientated French Language Style.

In Nova Scotia (Saskatchewan too),
Beauchemin's *Le Matou* is *The Alley Cat,*
and the cat wants to be Maurice Richard
but Timothy Eaton was really mean.

The Eaton Centre in Toronto (note
bizarre Canadian spelling of *center*)
is still my favourite Eaton Centre of all,
a setting in my novel, *La Bière Perdue.*

**A la mémoire de moi-même et M. de Fenouillet et le
burger 'W' chez Wendy's.**

Far from the Fina gas station of your youth –
not teaching in that New England College
dreamed of in grad school – walking Jean Talon,
looking for a reasonable soup, you're done.

Under the radiant lamps of Rona,
you picked out things as if being watched
by that married woman in Chicago
who had opinions on bathroom fixtures.

You're the subject in an undergraduate
poem, appearing as 'fat and crying,'
but, importantly, you inspire the speaker
to never listen to her stupid boyfriend.

In Wendy's, in Les Galeries D'Anjou,
you received the Thousand Island Dressing
of Life! In the sun by the house your father built,
you had the wing of faith - the whole spicy bird.

(*after Crémazie*)

As the editor of the *Fiddlehead* once asked me, 'Have you even tried writing poems that make no mention of arena football star Jared Lorenzen or that time you brought a Shamrock Shake to a job interview?'

It was the most profound educational
experience I could ever imagine.
I'm speaking, of course, of the 'How to Stop
Wanting Love' entry on WikiHow.

So what, polynut? I had time for nachos.
From ballpark nachos and up the ladder
to 7-Eleven nachos and, then,
the kind of nachos Gandhi would make.

Men like me were not meant to write poems
and threaten to jump off a city bridge.
Men like me were meant to change your oil
and quietly jump off a city bridge.

Too destroyed to know sexy underwear,
I still fit in most places. Perhaps not
Shakira concerts (Shakira hates that),
but I recognized the world as normal.

We should all thank Taylor Swift for taking on what poets so often vaingloriously try (and fail) to express and how she, rather than being intimidated by such endeavour, gives appropriate expression to the most motivating human sentiments and puts it all into catchy, heartfelt songs.

If I were to wear your little red square
it would be to commemorate the death
of a dear friend, and if that friend's name
were Reddinger 'LaRouge' Crimsonforce.

If I were to express my best days with you
of course I'd mention the shrimp croquettes
but I'd earn my poet's pay in images
of a hurt man trying to talk to a truck.

If I were to go back in time it would be
just before whoever wrote 'If I Could
Turn Back Time' for Cher, but I would still
come back with a poem much like this.

If I were to sleep all day, I'd give it all
to you and you'd get remarried, remarried
like you used to do! Like you used to chew
licorice red, mon petit squarehead.

I was always told a good Canadian poet should only publish once a year, on the Queen's birthday, and on the subject of the Queen's birthday.

A government program seeks to leave poems
in hospital waiting rooms so patients
might read them and begin to understand
there are worse things than diabetes.

When Seamus Heaney passed away, he took
his 'Seven Secret Words that Rhyme with Horse'
to the grave with him. Our rented horse-drawn hearse
just clopped away, Canadian *cloppe après cloppe.*

Editions of Gwendolyn MacEwen
where the word *love* is purposely crossed out
and replaced with the word *Kahlua* –
are those still considered *erasures*?

Show, don't tell. Show everyone in Mimico
the kind of mustard-coloured activewear
one only sees in the best golf magazines –
the kind they used to have in waiting rooms.

Do you like it when I call you Snoodlepuss, Snoodlepuss?

I'm going to pretend your poem was in French,
and 'The soul of an egg / salad sandwich
bought from / the Pentagon's automat'
was about falling asleep on my shoulder.

I'm going to look a series of websites
in the eye and tell them I won't back down,
and I will, by nighttime, start typing up
the story that puts the *pro* in *protagonist*.

I was aware of all your peculiar
ailments. Canapé Rash. Top Hat Dropsy.
Turtle Soup Intolerance. Limousine
Anxiety. It's amazing you survived.

I wanted to ask about your silk allergies.
To see if you were coping. Just to see
if you still write poems about Bigfoot
and if that Bigfoot has an Irish name.

Every time a poet is denied a council grant, a blind child is given back the power of sight.

Seems a shame I spent about seven years
saying things that were not dissimilar
to what Beyoncé says in 'Halo' – except
without the beauty of Beyoncé's words.

When I failed, my mother liked to say,
'You are all the man you ever will be.'
Meaning you can't just wait to get better.
Don't just lie there in a ditch you dug.

Oh, I could not keep my story straight.
Did I walk out from a fiery plane crash?
Was it cool being ambassador to Spain?
Did Philip Larkin really call me 'dudebro'?

I won't say I found a hole so dark
I understood it as an abscess of hell.
I'll just say I started watching *Frasier*.
I'll just say 'every single episode.'

I was advised to call your betrayal something other than *betrayal* so I am going to call your betrayal your *Toyota Camry*.

Someone is learning accordion downstairs.
Why even live in Canada if moose
never destroy the tasteful apartments
of hipsters playing the accordion?

I felt more alone when you still lived here,
so watching a mouse skitter in the kitchen
or getting up to eat Count Chocula
over the sink are not things that sadden me.

Perhaps the hyperbole proves a point:
your Toyota Camry made a statement.
I'm frankly amused I still do normal things,
your Toyota Camry once hurt so much.

If I found an accordion, just before
bringing it to a pawn shop, I'd squeeze out
a few bars of that song I think you liked,
happy I could, at least, make it sound awful.

**There's no official bird of Canada but if there were it
would be a bird that could write letters to the editor
about how it thinks pelicans are fat.**

There were Elizabeth Bishop buttercups
and a few Elizabeth Bishop daisies.
There was Donk's 'The Otter's Deposition'
and Fatchett's 'Sestina for a Tendril.'

Most poems were Toronto apartments,
though, and the trope of Winnipeg snows
was as rare as a Leonard Cohen sighting
outside chez Les Bobards in Montreal.

Nineteenth-century American lit
is more awkward than Canadian lit
because it didn't have the example
of twentieth-century America.

Canada had fuckable trees, spruce and larch,
but it also had baseball and ketchup hearts.
Our prime ministers looked at all the birds,
grateful every one was not a poem.

The Canada Goose is symbolic of 'a desire to escape problems,' particularly if your problem is that you live in Canada.

Four years since my last passport photo.
If I had to name one exclusive thing
that has irrevocably harmed my life
I'd say it was my physical appearance.

The ugly should never leave their hometown.
Hometown friends will tell you, 'You're killin' it,
Smokey Smokestack!,' but strangers will just stare,
hoping you slip back to the Black Lagoon.

My passport has fewer barbecue stains
than some people think. You'd have to know me
to see my gold teeth, have me tell you
how I got that nasty scar on my cheek.

I learned a lot about love in my life.
Not the going-to-Yankee-Stadium-
with-Kate-Upton kind of learning, mind you,
nothing that would demand a quote from Donne.

Canadian poet Gwendolyn MacEwen kept four wrens in her apartment in Toronto, once even sewing little Beatles outfits for them.

Daily, I curl into whatever fries
and curd combination keeps me alive,
and by alive I just mean witlessly
reply-tweeting to Alyssa Milano.

I'm not saying I suddenly got too old.
I was too old years ago. That was clear
when I started buying things – anything –
that promised cheap relief of ankle pain.

My mother would cry if she knew how
much money I waste on taxis. I pray
I get through lunch without hearing someone
say, 'I, the Duke of Poetry, spit on you!'

I cry when I listen to those country songs
written at the height of the Iraq War.
I mean, those are the only things that ever
move me to tears now that my friends are gone.

Alexander Mackenzie was the first of Canada's prime ministers to be attacked and eaten by owls.

So, I think about how it all went wrong,
when, really, that should be as obvious
as wondering why a horse can't string a guitar
or why there are so few poems about NASCAR.

I'm fifty-two now, yet wisdom eludes me –
unless falling asleep at a Wendy's
to dream about a time where I would not
fall deep asleep at a Wendy's is wise.

Getting mad at you for not loving me
is like being mad at Saturn for not
having an IKEA to buy cheap shelves
for my mint copies of *Spy* magazine.

So, the regret is about connection,
but not the icky way you meant *connection* –
I mean iPhone, I mean, in retrospect,
I'm grateful you never once stabbed me.

Ornithologists believe the 'laughing seagull' is laughing at blackbirds for that stupid Beatles song about them.

When I turn and say I 'hate' the Beatles,
don't get me wrong. I don't mean it that way.
I just mean that I hate their horrible
music. That's it. Just their horrible music.

When I think of the Beatles' hit songs –
from 'Oopie Doopie Bee' to 'O Deirdre,'
from 'Mrs. Medwin's Sunday Chutney'
to 'Step Right Up, Sidney Dear' – I wince.

Not because their songs are poorly written
or performed in an inadequate fashion.
For a group so drug-addled they could not
perform live, the Beatles made hit records!

It just makes me wince. Maybe that's just me.
I've seen people singing classic Beatles songs –
from 'Hey, Moon Cat!' to 'Love Is So Lovely' –
and they all seemed perfectly happy to me.

The Fonzie-Swans at Coole.

My creative writing teacher would say,
'You fool, I said *pellucid* not *lucid*!'
Professor Manifesto, hands on hips,
said, 'You should write more about my travels.'

I started writing observationals:
a stiff moon in the church's parking lot,
Professor Manifesto yells, 'You suck,
stiff moon!,' however manifesto-y.

Those are some sexy apostles, that's true.
But those were also some hot-assed Pharisees.
When will it get so warm I won't want to drink
a venti non-fat pumpkin-spiced latté?

I love you, Professor Manifesto!
You told me I'd regret the day I said,
'Better a smudge of Doritos dust
than a week in the Bodleian with you.'

'You talk like we shouldn't be pelting you with wet sacks of garbage.'

So far out in the Mojave Desert
there are only two radio stations:
Christian and Christian Pop. I air guitar
the tune to 'It's Chilltown, My Chill Saviour.'

Choosing *chili verde* or *colorado*
would have destroyed Solomon. Should I die
because I can't choose between a mirror
and a better, more cost-effective, mirror?

If you put a massive lump of grey hair
on a potato you wouldn't be able
to distinguish it from me. Potato,
do potato, re potato, mi, so, fa.

Though the dust I hear about Bro Vegas
and that the ex is killing it at Keno;
a granite mountain gives up many stones,
'O Totes Cool Lord, You're Terribly Awesome.'

**If you can't handle me when I'm wearing my Van Halen
T-shirt, you don't deserve me when I'm wearing my other
Van Halen T-shirt.**

If you were there that night at McSwink's,
when I proclaimed, 'As God is my witness,
I'll never mix Sprite and brandy again!'
you may want to skip over this poem.

You may want to accept as blanket
the apologies I offer to those
I mocked for their weaved-leather belts
and dubbed the Weaved-Leather Belt Circle.

The WLBC was nice to me
and, into Lassie, I was glad enough
to lecture about Lassie at McSwink's,
reading poems I thought Lassie would like.

At some point, you realize validation
is just some toothless editor saying,
'Looks like somebody special's going to find
a World War One helmet in their stocking!'

When Sylvia Plath said, 'People or stars regard me sadly,' I think she mostly meant 'people.'

Poetry's not hard. All you have to do is,
instead of saying things like 'I washed my clothes
at a motel laundromat in Orchard Park,
NY,' say, 'I ate gold in Milan.'

Tell it slant. You don't have to use old-fashioned
phrases like 'Write down Prince John a villain!'
Just imagine you're at a seminar
with Prince John, making fun of fat people.

Show don't tell. Don't say, 'My feelings were hurt
when you all called me bottom-lining trash' -
that's telling. Say, 'You all have such great taste
in cinema!' – it shows with fewer words.

Make it new. You learn from the old masters,
taking Keats's 'I believe you had liked me
for my own sake' and renewing it
to 'Wanna do a panel at AWP?'

NOTEBOOK IV

LES CHANSONS D'ANJOU

'Don't be fooled by my metafiction in the
Massachusetts Review / I'm still Dave from Anjou.'

Some like The Mists of Avalon *with a little extra mist*
Some put the 'All right!' in oreillies de crisse
But I love noodles

Some love a book gloriously vain and shortsighted
Some must ask the Pointer Sisters if they're truly excited
But I love noodles

Some ask Sexy Jesus, 'What happened to my sexy life?'
Some fall asleep to episodes of McMillan and Wife
But I love noodles

Some like to walk in beauty like the night
Some like to wear the same big glasses as Judith Light
But I love noodles

Some like a mountaintop to compose poems sublime
Some dream of a Bomb Pop lemon, banana and lime
But I love noodles

Unfuckable is the new thirty.

Coneflowers like a dirty taffeta,
purple daisies like dirt, dirty knobs of phlox,
dirtfuck hollyhocks, scarred up and dead-sauced,
stuck in an apartment in a heat wave.

What, dear flower, was poetry good for
besides putting the capitalist force
of college diplomas into the phrase
'If you don't love me I'm gonna kill myself'?

The wise take being unloved as given,
saying, 'Smell the hyssop syrup,' or some such:
whipping biscuits off a hotel rooftop,
hollerin', 'Hyacinths symbolize baseball!'

Primrose like something prim, the way a smudge
of colour is as good as it will get.
The way one hands out rue like sunscreen
'cause it's going to be one of those Sundays.

Beautiful fat pants.

Beautiful fat pants, today is our day.
No pretending to read *I, Seamus Heaney*,
no Skyping with pretendfriend.com.
Beautiful fat pants, beautiful fat pants.

Beautiful fat pants, you remember me.
The reruns of *Moesha*, the noodle soups,
the new poetry of Suzanne McNews.
Beautiful fat pants, beautiful fat pants.

Beautiful fat pants never killed a goose.
Steelsmith for all of Absentmind Township,
shepherd through the purply Valley of Chafe.
Beautiful fat pants, beautiful fat pants.

Beautiful fat pants, today will be smooth.
The indoors bulge with Internet quilting,
desktop flowers made up of Twitter barbs.
Beautiful fat pants, beautiful fat pants.

Lullaby: People will like you better after you're dead.

I tell jokes to my doctor. Not the kind
about a french fry who's dating ketchup,
but the jokes I put on twitter just before
I'm unfollowed by @IAmSexyBookstore.

'Do you think I will still heal if I drink Sprite?'
He doesn't even laugh, adjusts the X-ray,
until he finally avers, 'Of course! Sure!'
I'm not dying, I should add. Just broken.

A swollen ankle hate-fucked a kidney.
My doctor thinks I'm kidding when I ask,
'Who will put up pictures of cheeseburgers
on my Facebook if I'm out of commish?'

Who will attend my life's dropping hours?
The thousands of razors I've saved, thinking,
'I'll just let this go. Sooner or later
you're gonna have to call me Santa Claus.'

Beef-borne illness.

If I were to die of a beef-borne illness,
a beef-born illness, a beef-borne illness;
if I were to die of a beef-borne illness,
I'd hope you would die from it too.

If I named my daughter Beef Borne Illness,
Beef Borne Illness, Beef Borne Illness;
if I named my daughter Beef Borne Illness,
I bet you she could handle her booze.

If I summered by Lake Beef Borne Illness,
Lake Beef Borne Illness, Lake Beef Borne Illness;
if I summered by Lake Beef Borne Illness,
I would discover a better way to drown.

So if you ever sing of beef-borne illness,
beef-born illness, beef-borne illness;
if you ever sing of beef-borne illness,
it will be like you're not making a sound.

Song for a house arrest.

This is the ankle bracelet, John Keats,
that beeps whenever you go to Wendy's.
This is the barrel of onion soup mix
they give you for calling yourself trash.

Which character will you relate to now?
Which literary character will it be?
The Elvis character in *Roustabout*
or the Elvis character in *Tickle Me*?

This is no lights after curfew, Rimbaud.
This is to hell with a once-cherished cause.
Very few walk up to the guillotine
still shouting, '*Vive la révolution!*'

Which character will you relate to now?
Which literary character will it be?
The Elvis character in *Kissin' Cousins*
or the Elvis character in *Blue Hawaii*?

Anthem for why you write poetry.

You do it for indie bands and pop-up
brunches. You do it for every person
who filled in that Ten Books meme on Facebook,
careful to include books they sort of read.

You do it for the graduates who moved
to Vancouver and then rarely, if ever,
fail to use the word 'gentrification.'
You do it for Occupy Oakville.

You do it for the teacher who said, once,
he had drinks with Elizabeth Wurtzel.
You do it for microcrafted microbrew,
for speeches about 'the community.'

You do it in the hope that one fine day
they will stop calling you fat and stupid
because, really, take a look at yourself.
You do it for every cat named Salinger.

Power ballad in a convex mirror.

My lectures lost their steam over time,
but Snooki said it best in her podcast:
'A duel gets increasingly formal
up until the last exchange of fire.'

Once my frontyard sparrows and frontyard wrens
became *Tuscan sparrows* and *Tuscan wrens*,
I was publishable! No stepping back
once I put that ointment on that old itch.

All lectures die the moment you say, 'Now,
turn to page' whatever. Whatever page,
I was by the window looking out for
the AuCoq car with its AuCoq chicken.

Finding out that people care would be like
finding out the moon runs on Chevron Oil.
Surprising, but then maybe worth noting
I was paraphrasing the quote from Snooki.

Our Parnassus will go on.

The great poets are always decisive.
When Sylvia Plath went for chicken wings,
she never had to think twice about whether
to order them Mild, Hot or Suicide.

When Edward 'Ted' Hughes would buy summer shorts,
he could hear the the hair on his legs touch
and the hairs would sing 'MMMBop' in Welsh.
Such are the legs of Legsy the Poet.

But hey, leg up when the editor lags:
'We're not looking for *work* but for *content* –
just a thing that frames pictures of Yaddo,
a thing that says, 'I don't *rent* tuxedos!'

When the great poets think upon the sun
they must surely think of Mr. Drummond,
dropping to one knee, outstretching his arms,
as if anything were possible with love.

Schoolhouse Lilies

Except when he was watching baseball,
it seemed my father was always outdoors,
tipping his hat to locals, watering
the flowers that focused his retirement.

A Yankees fan for over ninety years,
in mid-September, a week before he died,
my father said the retiring Derek Jeter
was 'too old to play short. They need home runs!'

My father grew rows of spider flowers
but he called them by their French name, *cleomes*.
The cleomes were gone by mid-October
and the Yankees didn't make the playoffs.

Some call oxblood lilies *schoolhouse lilies*
because when they bloom it's time to go back.
'It's good to have a job,' my father told me,
as I complained about ever returning.

Acknowledgements

'The abuse we have taken, and the abuse we must be prepared to take for the entire winter, we richly deserve.' – Boston Red Sox shortstop Rick Burleson, in 1978, upon once again losing to the New York Yankees.

Some of the poems (or versions of them) in this collection have previously appeared in *Canadian Literature*, Canadian Poetries, Cosmonaut Avenue, Dusie, *Fjords*, Hazlitt, *The Heart of the Order: Baseball Poems*, Jacket2, *Language Matters: Interviews with 22 Quebec Poets*, Lemon Hound, the *Literary Review of Canada*, *Matrix*, McSweeney's, NewPoetry, *OTP 2*, *Poetry is Dead*, the *Toronto Quarterly*, Queen Mob's Teahouse, the *Walrus*, the *Washington Square Journal* and *Window Fishing: The Night We Caught Beatlemania*. 'The History of Baseball' served initially as text for visual art by Matthew Thompson, Aanchal Molhotra and the TANDEM art team at the Mouse Print Gallery in Montreal during April of 2013. I would like to thank the generous assistance of the Canada Council for the Arts.

Merci, merci millefois to the entire Coach House team, esp. my editor, Jeramy Dodds, and to the always amazing and insightful Alana Wilcox. Grateful acknowledgements to Elizabeth Bachinsky, Arjun Basu, Jeremy Breen, Jason Camlot, Steve Creep, Lynn Crosbie, Jon Paul Fiorentino, Deanna Fong, Sara Johnston, Scott Macdonald, Alessandro Porco, Bükem Reitmayer, Robin Richardson, Matthew Rosenberg, Jacob Spector, Mike Spry, Andrea Stevens and Sarah Steinberg. Special thanks to Dave Kaufman for my tenure as 'the poet laureate of CJAD radio' in Montreal and for giving me airtime to premiere many of these poems (or, at least, some of the funnier lines) on *The Exchange*. Love to everyone in my family, Johnny, Gail and Heather and all their families; to Janice and Mike keeping it real in Ville D'Anjou and, most of all, to Carol and 'The Team.' #ILoveNoodles

J'suis tellement fancy
Gatorade mojitos
Banni de Wendy's
Les Promenades de St. Bruno

David McGimpsey was born and raised in Montreal. He is the author of several volumes of poetry, including the collection of sonnets *Li'l Bastard,* which was named a book of the year by both the *National Post* and the *Quill and Quire* and was a finalist for Canada's Governor General's Award. David is also the author of the short fiction collection *Certifiable* and the award-winning critical study *Imagining Baseball: America's Pastime and Popular Culture.* He is a musician, a fiction editor for Joyland, and his travel writing is a regular feature of *EnRoute* magazine. Named by the CBC as one of the 'Top Ten English language poets in Canada,' his work was also the subject of the book of essays *Population Me: Essays on David McGimpsey.* A PhD in American Literature, David teaches at Concordia University.

PREVIOUS BOOKS
Li'l Bastard
Sitcom
Certifiable
Hamburger Valley, California
Imagining Baseball: America's Pastime and Popular Culture
Dogboy
Lardcake

Typeset in Warnock and Gibson.

Printed at the old Coach House on bpNichol Lane in Toronto, Ontario, on Zephyr Antique Laid paper, which was manufactured, acid-free, in Saint-Jérôme, Quebec, from second-growth forests. This book was printed with vegetable-based ink on a 1965 Heidelberg KORD offset litho press. Its pages were folded on a Baumfolder, gathered by hand, bound on a Sulby Auto-Minabinda and trimmed on a Polar single-knife cutter.

Edited by Jeramy Dodds
Designed by Alana Wilcox
Cover image: *Shy Anne*, from a Fad of the Month Club postcard produced by the National Handcraft Institute of Des Moines, February 1967. Every effort has been made to contact the copyright holder for their permission to reproduce this image. Coach House would be grateful to hear from the copyright holder and will undertake to acknowledge them in future editions of the book.

Coach House Books
80 bpNichol Lane
Toronto ON M5S 3J4 Canada

416 979 2217
800 367 6360

mail@chbooks.com
www.chbooks.com